CW00867333

# A little corner of paradise

**by Helen-Anne Shields**

Copyright © Helen-Anne Shields - 2015

Texts by Helen-Anne Shields
Watercolors by Pascal Margat
Page layout & illustrations by Véronique Bonnel

Published by Auld Alliance Contemporary Exhibitions (AACE)

*No part of this book may be reproduced or transmitted in any form or
by any other means without permission in writing from the publisher,
except by a reviewer who wishes to quote brief passages in connection
with a review written for insertion in a magazine, newspaper or broadcast*

For Peter and Bridget

# FIRST ARRIVALS

## 17 August

We arrived in a deafening uproar on that warm summer's night. Continuous strings of rain were dropping vertically from the black night and rebounding on the gravel driveway and scanty, sunburnt lawn, soaking our sandaled feet. The clouds crashed and exploded, zigzags of lightening lit up the night sporadically, as they do so well in the South of France. No-one except we four in the car were out on that night. But the house we came to was alive.

The thick stone walls were almost invisible in the night storm, but light poured out from the glass panel of the main doorway, and upstairs, a row of smiling yellow rectangles lit up our arrival from the children's rooms. Opening the car doors, our expressions fleeting between pleasure and grimaces at this welcome homecoming in the driving rain, we could hear a chorus of our names: "Helen, Helen! Caitlin, Caitlin!".

Every one of the golden-haired children was on the upstairs balcony, balls of pure energy jumping up and down, getting soaked in the rain, shouting our names with joy at the top of their lungs: "Caitlin, Helen" – bang, crash, flash – "Helen, Caitlin".

The parents, Daniel and Holly had appeared at the now open doorway, beckoning us in, and the noise continued as we tried under an umbrella to exchange phone numbers with the girls who had been so good as to give us a lift from the train station in Cahors along the tortuous banks of the River Lot through the slashing rain to our destination at Tour de Faure. And then the car was gone, and we were in the warmth of the sitting-room surrounded by the family, so pleased to be back in their midst.

That warmest of welcomes on that terrible stormy night has remained ever-engraved in my memory. The children are now many years older, but nothing of that first summer has dissipated. I think it is true that every house holds its own special feelings. When we enter a house we know if we will be happy to spend time there or if instead it will make us feel creepy or sad. The house in Tour de Faure is impregnated with happy feelings. I do not know if that feeling was there before the Warner family bought the house, or if it is their aura that has seeped into the walls. Whatever the case, that is the way it is now - the warmth of the family and the weather are imprinted forever in my heart, and in the walls of that house. These are the feelings that come to me whenever I think of Tour de Faure, its yellow sunflowers, wooded hills, and the Lot's beautiful cosy valley.

My story of the Lot is this story of warmth, of geographical and historical beauty, of fresh air and sun and fun, of friendships and families.

Let us go back a few days in time, to my very first arrival in the Lot. The above arrival took place a few days later after a couple of days away visiting Toulouse.

My first holiday in the Lot came about by chance. I arrived in France to set up a new life directly from my old life in Scotland. I just happened to be befriended by another Scottish girl living in Paris who took me under her wing, a new foreigner in France, and brought me to the South West, to the old and peaceful village of Tour de Faure, and to the Warner family's summer home. There is nothing in that holiday that clashed or banged, except the spectacular thunderstorm I have already told you about. It was a perfect holiday.

Caitlin and I arrived that first day on a beautifully warm and sunny summer's day. Daniel, our host, picked us up from the train in Cahors, Caitlin feeling that perhaps she should not have bothered him on his holiday, but loath to get the bus with all our sack and pack.

My first impression of him was of a genteel but laid-back man. He is tall and bearded, a successful product from an adolescence spent in the 60s, relaxed and friendly, intelligent and open to the world and whatever it might have to offer.

Like myself, he is also a bookworm and over the summers that we have now shared this house with the Warner family, we have always talked of books; if we borrow the house in their absence, several are always left for me in the wardrobe in their bedroom.

Daniel spends each summer holiday sitting in his particular place at the wooden table in the shade of the pergola on the patio, reading. It has become a custom over the years to drive past the house and look back over our shoulders to be sure that Daniel is there. He has always been there. He has never disappointed us. And having spotted him, my partner, Pascal, and I look at each other with immense satisfaction in our smiles. Some things never change. Some things never should change.

But on my very first day in the Lot, I did not know any of this yet. The family, the house, the Lot still had to be discovered.

By the time I got to Tour de Faure from the station in Cahors I had probably already fallen in love with the Lot. The summer weather is sublime, all golden sunshine and blue skies, but nevertheless the vegetation remains green. The drive from Cahors to Tour de Faure is memorable for the beautiful scenery: the River Lot as it flows steadily through its valley is interspersed with weirs of fast-flowing white water. On one side white cliffs and wooded hillsides dominate the river, with flat agricultural lands growing sunflowers, corn or asparagus on the other.

The tortuous road leads us under overhanging cliffs or through tunnels cut out of them. We always whoop out of the windows when we drive through the sudden coolness of the tunnels to hear ourselves echo. We pass quaint ancient villages, skinny bridges, semi-troglodyte houses cut out of the cliffs and spot St Cirq Lapopie perched on top of its hill, with its steep, red-tiled roofs, typical of the region, as we near Tour de Faure.

Upon arrival at the sprawling old house, I meet the rest of the family.

Holly is a softly-spoken mother of five, and with this household of free-range children to feed, and look after, not to mention horses, sheep, and cats, she can turn her hand to anything that will keep the house turning clockwise, and the children with it. She does this with a quiet confidence sometimes lost on her husband.

Now, many years later, Daniel and Holly have another child, Sam. Pascal and I would like to be four again and have stories read to us in his father's full-bodied, warm voice. Daniel could definitely have rivalled Richard Burton on stage.

Since that first meeting, Pascal and I have often borrowed the house from our friends the Warners, and we invite our friends to come and join us. It is a big house with five bedrooms and very importantly has a pool room, where we have had years of fun in after-dinner tournaments. This all sounds decidedly elegant doesn't it; but in fact it is not. The house is a perfect holiday house. It has everything and more that you might need in the form of rooms, kitchen equipment, games to play, bicycles, canoes, space; but it is one of those old French farmhouses, which has not yet been completely refurbished. It is therefore not a place where children have to worry about limiting the number of times they run in and out, wiping their feet.

## This summer
## Day 1

### Tour de Faure

I love this moment of peace and relative coolness in the early morning shade. My moment of solitude before the household wakes up. The five bedrooms are choc-a-bloc full after the arrival of friends from Scotland, the ages of children varying from Daisy at 7 to Charlie at 16. And then we four adults: Alex and Rosie; Pascal and I.

Pascal has been up for hours already, two instant coffees drunk, half a book read, and now he has gone to his habitual place at the camping site café, the Camping de la Plage, near the river for his morning doze of strongly caffeinated espresso. Oscar, our Westie, has gone off with him for his morning walk before it gets too hot for his fur-coated body. They will stop off at the boulangerie on their way back up the hill home – primarily in the hope of a smile from the boulangère – secondly to ensure a supply of fresh, warm baguettes for our friends.

I wonder if Daniel knows I take his special place at the table when he is not here... at his usual place at the big wooden table here on the veranda, reading.

I can see that the hills coming down from the Causses (the plateau that tops the valley of the Lot river, classified as a National Park: the "Parc naturel régional des Causses de Quercy") opposite are as beautifully green as ever. It never ceases to amaze me in the hot, dry summer months that the leaves keep their colour. The sun has not quite made it over the Causses yet, but I feel it getting closer as the temperature rises. The cicadas can feel it too. They are already singing frantically among the vegetation lining the field opposite the house…

The field is high in grass. I can see that the grass feels the heat too, dry and yellowing off. The local tractor-owner who mows it will come soon, then the children will be able to play there without fear of snakes biting their ankles.

I always like to retrace the footsteps of my first ever stay in the Lot when I am here, and I allow my memories to come.

My Scottish friend, Caitlin, showed me around on foot, and it was a pleasure to discover all the little details of the village, like only a village child would normally know. Caitlin was a walker. Was this due to having no transport of her own? Or was it a habit? I will probably never know as Caitlin has now moved from France to the antipodes. But whatever the reason, that first summer was spent on foot. We walked all over the village of Tour de Faure and the surrounding area, something I loved and I have therefore tried to instil in every visitor since - but with little success. Most people prefer the car, or the bicycles, even if the seats are so old your bottom already feels like it has been sawn in half by the time you get to the base of the hill. Yes, the hill.

The house is the last on a steep gravel track going up into the wooded hills beyond. There is a field across from the house, one neighbouring house lower down the track can be seen from the terrace, and above that only trees.

On the one hand, it is lovely to be so well away from everything. We like the isolation and the possibility that brings to play music really, really, really loudly without it bothering anyone, and have many friends for long, typically French dinners outside with no neighbours to overhear or be upset by the noise. Isolation gives freedom.

On the other hand, the great thing about the house in Tour de Faure is that you also have everything that isolation cannot usually provide – just at the bottom of the hill is the boulangerie with the boulangère and her apparently lovely smile, and the épicerie, the river, the "beach", the fruit and vegetable stall near the camping ground, a couple of cafés and restaurants - all within easy walking distance.

However, as I said, only Caitlin and I liked to walk. Pascal can be persuaded sometimes, which means Olivier who is still only 14, gets roped in too - no choice at 14. No driving licence. Oh to be a grown up! The problem is, whatever locomotion you use unless it is the car – foot, bicycle, skateboard - the problem is that hill. You have to come back up it again!

Pure laziness? Not necessarily. It is true that in the boiling 40 degree August sun, a lack of physical exertion, moreover with an open window letting the breeze in or even better although not ecologically so, air conditioning, the car is an attractive option.

On that very first day in Tour de Faure, we walked down the hill in the heat, wearing summer dresses and sunhats. We passed by various old, stone houses, cool in their thick walls, interspersed with fields full of beautiful sunflowers.

Today there is wheat gently waving in the warm breeze in those same fields, some of it flattened from a sudden storm.

Nearing the bottom of the hill we turned left towards the centre of the village. We pass the tennis court and the library, then a few old stone houses.

There, if you look carefully you can still make out a line of arched facades, which used to be shop entrances, but have now been sealed up and replaced by windows. One used to be the butcher shop; now there is a travelling butcher.

Indeed, as in many villages in France, and no doubt throughout the industrialised world, all of the little shops close down and the big monopolies take over.

At the end of the little row of arcades and stone houses, we come into the village square. Here we can hear the ding dong from the nearby church clock-tower, which tolls every hour from 8am.

My friends in the village, Marcel and Odette, told me that when the bell-tower was being built around 1850, they found a stone engraved with a date from the fifth century inside a stone coffin. This coffin was surrounded by others in the middle of an ancient cemetery, which proves that it was a place of worship long before the present church stood here.

In my imagination, I make the few steps across the village square and round toward the Tour. I always like walking up to that part of the village. On my first holiday here I had fallen in love with the building with the round towers. Old, dilapidated buildings always fire my imagination. Since then, it has been spruced up and some of the rooms can be rented. However, rumour has it that it is not this building with the rounded towers that gives the village its name. It is the square-towered house that does that. According, once again, to Marcel, Odette and the rumour, this square tower gave its name to the village because the demoiselles de Faure used to live in it. Before 1902 the village was annexed to St Cirq Lapopie, the medieval town, now classed as a historical monument, which dominates the valley from its perch above the river and Tour de Faure.

\*\*\*

As our friends begin to arrive at the breakfast table, smiling and still sleepy, full of plans for the first day of their holiday, discussed over coffee and warm baguette supplied by Pascal, I realise I will have to follow the old adage: "When you have invited friends to join you on holiday, do what the friends want"... Personally I would have preferred our first day to be a lazy one, spent down by the campsite at the river at the sandy "beach" or at our secret pebbled beach out past the lock. But instead we gratified the needs of our friends.

# Pech Merle
## Prehistoric Cave

Discovered in 1922 by André David (16 years old) and Henri Dutertre (15); open to the public since 1926; rediscovered via Internet one month ago by ever-organised Rosie before she even set foot in the Lot Valley, and pre-booked via telephone all the way from Scotland. All this in order to satisfy her nine year old son's need for anything even vaguely related to prehistoric monsters.

All nine of us, except Pascal and Oscar (no dogs allowed), who stayed above ground in the kind 28°C morning heat to paint and pant, respectively, made our way down the steps (cut out in 1923) to the cool of the prehistoric caves (in existence since long before 1923). Imagine all those years ago, prehistoric man, in the search for their equivalent of canvas, squeezed in through a tunnel and crawled along in the pitch black, not knowing what giant insect might lie in wait. And what about rats! All that to paint animals (very well); and to paint human beings (very badly) on the cave walls. Why is it that prehistoric woman is depicted with a very small head (no brain presumably), a very large bottom and a stomach bearing quintuplets? Whereas prehistoric man is much more proportional.

Imagine that 25 000 years later, modern man (or teenager in this case) squeezed in through the same tunnel, in the same darkness, with a possibly greater aversion to insects than his predecessor. This time to look at the paintings.

Our group showed definite signs of our varying ages: Cameron, Harry and Daisy, our three under twelves, were extremely interested in everything they saw: beautiful stalactites and sta-lagmites, and perfectly formed spinning tops, all made naturally over thousands of years by dripping water; there was the scratch of an ancient bear's claws in its lair; a 10 000-year-old human footprint; and the wonderful handprints and paintings of horses, bears, bison, aurochs, and mammoths.

There was also a lion... I found that confusing. Did lion's live in France 10-25 000 years ago? Had prehistoric man already travelled to Africa...? I'm sure the answer to that lies somewhere on Internet...

The most recent of these paintings was about 10 000 years old; the oldest around 25 000 years old. Olivier and Charlie, our two adolescents, however, could not decide whether it was cool to find such things interesting or not. This was obvious from their overly-relaxed, hands-in-pockets slouch.

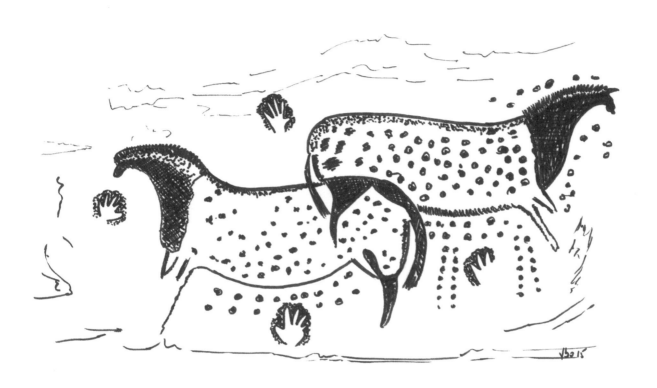

As a tree lover, one of my favourite discoveries on this new first day in the caves at Pech Merle was the amazing tree root that traverses the four metres of rock from the surface, to make its way into the cool of the caves. The root hangs about another eight metres from the ceiling to the floor of the cave, and then disappears into the next level of rock beneath our feet. Apparently nobody has ever tried to find out just how far towards the earth's centre it travels. When we came back up to the surface and the heat hit us to remind us that it was summer, we found the tree: a triple-trunked oak.

Perhaps I can persuade Pascal to paint it...

# This summer – Day 2

## St Cirq Lapopie

Today we killed two birds with one stone. First, we satisfied Rosie's paramount necessity: shopping. And second, to compensate my need to use my own locomotion, we walked (rather than took the car) up to St Cirq Lapopie.

St Cirq Lapopie is a little medieval gem perched up high on its hilltop (about 100m above the Lot river). In fact it won the most beautiful village in France TV award in 2012. St Cirq dominates the valley and our village of Tour de Faure on the opposite shore. Under its protection, at the shoreline of the river lie the camping ground with its "beach", the disused towpath, which is now simply an interesting path to walk along from the foot of St Cirq to the village of Bouziès, and there is also our secret pebbled beach. From the riverside looking up, walking up to the village appears to be quite a feat, but Pascal and I have discovered a couple of little pathways through green foliage that make the climb relatively easy. On this second day, we took the path that passes by a little hidden chapel nestled on the side of the hill. This is not the only religious hideaway among the trees of the Causses. Indeed while walking in the hills we have occasionally come across scallop shells, indicating the way to the nearest chapel on the Way of St James (Chemins de Saint-Jacques-de-Compostelle).

The pathways up to St Cirq Lapopie are easy to miss amongst the vegetation, just before the old towpath. Everyone was relieved to arrive quicker than they had anticipated, except Alex who, used to jogging every morning whatever the temperature, could have easily continued for a few more kilometres. I did not like to point out that this was only the beginning of the village - as the village is built on a steep hillside, they were in for a lot more climbing.

Our path brought us out into the village just above one of my favourite places in St Cirq – the château. St Cirq Lapopie is mainly made up of quaint 13th-15th century stone buildings. Often these are half-timbered houses where the wooden structural beams running between the stone is visible. The village makes an impressive picture from below, perched on its rock, and a very pretty picture from above with its steep, red-coloured flat-tile roofs, typical of the area, all squeezed closely together. Today we saw it from both angles.

Have you ever noticed that teenagers have no energy until they are forced to move. Then suddenly they have such an abundance that they run around like hares. As Rosie's Dad always said when she was a child, apparently, "Energy makes energy"… We had some very bouncy teenagers with us today.

We started off by following the cobbled streets to the château.

I have fond memories of the days when this château was owned by Mme Françoise Tournié and she opened it to the public for a very small amount of money. There you were allowed to discover her personal art collection or an occasional exhibition. Once we were lucky enough to spend a few moments with Mme Tournié who regaled us with stories of her youth and artist friends.

In fact St Cirq and the surrounding area were at one time the "in place" for prominent artists and writers: Henri Martin and André Breton to name just two of them.

Now this old château has found new owners and it has been turned into a luxurious bed and breakfast with a swimming pool cut deep and cool into the cliff.

From there, we walked up the steep slope, Oscar's four legs taking him up faster than we larger bipeds. Most of the roads house craft shops and restaurants, in their lovely stone-faceted buildings, so we visited as we roamed. Many of the old traditional crafts from St Cirq's hey-day have been conserved, for instance leatherwear, coppersmiths, wood turning or pottery. The latter two being my favourites. But there is much more too: jewellery, paintings, there is even a shop specialising only in witches. You have to look for it, though, parked down at the end of a little alleyway just where you might expect to find a witch bent over her cauldron, "Double, double toil and trouble; fire burn, and cauldron bubble".

Today, we were supposed to just look around and get ideas of what handcrafts we would like to take home with us...

But Rosie's hand is always close to her purse, so she came away with a beautiful lapis lazuli necklace. And I have to admit I bought some pottery items I have had my eye on for some time now too.

We dragged everyone all the way up to the ruins at the very top of the hill... the old chapel of St Cirq (Notre-Dame des Matelots)... where they set off the fireworks on the 15th of August. And where on this hot, sunny day the view out over the villages of St Cirq Lapopie, Tour de Faure, Bouziès and all the way down this beautiful valley is sublime.

One of the things I love about my little part of the Lot is that there is enough space to feel alone and free, but not enough to feel lonely. When looking out from this vantage point at the uppermost point of St Cirq Lapopie, the valley gives a feeling of protection. Just look around you - we are in a warm, green cocoon. We can see several villages dotted along the banks of the river and up on the Causses.

We are not alone. Yet, we are far from being suffocated.

There are green trees and fields between each village, so there is plenty of clean, unused air to breathe. There is a sense of freedom, autonomy, solitude; held together in the protective arms of the valley.

Some of the villages are built with the houses crammed together, like St Cirq or Bouziès, just a little downriver at the other end of the towpath. Then look across at Tour de Faure - there is a small centre, with the lovely old church, and its cemetery. There are a few houses there including the one that gave the village its name. But mostly it is spread out, farmland, interspersed with farmhouses in their typical regional style.

If you are looking for some company it is there at the neighbour's, at the boulangerie or the épicerie, in the one or two cafés, or one of the excellent restaurants. But you do not need to be bothered by people. They are close but yet so far.

No matter what the moment, there is always the right place to be.

## Le chemin de halage and Bouziès

At the foot of the rock on which St Cirq Lapopie stands lie many things: the sandy beach by the campsite, the Camping de la Plage, where you can happily take your children to swim under the watchful eye of the lifeguard, our hidden pebbled beach by the "écluse" (the lock), the mill where we have sat to watch many brilliant firework displays set off from Notre-Dame des Matelots at the highest point of St Cirq Lapopie on the day of Assumption. And there is also the "chemin de halage", the old towpath. The mill, weir, lock and the beautiful towpath remind us of the period of glory that St Cirq and the surrounding era once knew. Nowadays the towpath makes for a lovely walk between the foot of the hill at St Cirq and Bouziès, another quaint little village.

The beauty of the towpath between St Cirq and Bouziès is that it is chiselled out of the sheer rock face. Already the idea of horses on the towpath pulling boats along the river smacks of difficult days, where men were proud of their hard work. However, to make that possible, someone had to create the towpath out of the sheer rock of the white cliff. I can imagine those men from another time hammering their metal pegs into the rock face, their huge muscles flexing in the sun, sweat dripping from under their caps. There were no electric drills to make the work easier.

Oscar likes that walk because it is relatively cool between the rock and the water, and we come out into the shade of trees at Bouziès on the other side.

This year Pascal has repaired some of the old bicycles in the shed at the house and the boys (Pascal, Olivier and Charlie) accompanied me by bike. I left them, when we arrived in Bouziès, to cross by bicycle the hanging bridge and come back along the other side of the river, via tractor paths among the fields of sunflowers and corn; and I retraced my footsteps along the towpath with Oscar. (Albeit that Oscar is a dog, he never runs for too long, always being distracted by smells we humans would not appreciate, and therefore a hazardous companion for a bicycle ride). Unfortunately for Olivier the bumpy tractor path was too much for his ancient old bicycle and with a flat tyre, he had to push the bike all the way home. If you remember, there is also that hill to ascend to the house... That was the end of bicycles for Olivier.

Charlie's problem of the day was, in my opinion, greater than Olivier's. Today, as I was trying to have my moment of peace... Imagine... 7.30am, cool morning air after last night's spectacular thunderstorm, sitting in Daniel's favourite reading spot at the veranda table, sun just coming up over the causses, cicadas already singing their joy. Paradise. Without having had to go into our teenagers' room and do my usual wicked step-mother "Wakey-wakey, rise and shine!" call, here comes Charlie.

This being the first summer Olivier has brought a friend with him on holiday, and also the first time Charlie has met me, he has not dared to ask yet, what this wake-up call actually means.

Between you and I, I had heard that Charlie is not so good in English at school, so this was my warped way of trying to interest him in the subject. It will take him until the end of the holiday to get up the courage to ask. For the moment, he just looks at me in bewilderment: "Is she mad? Am I missing something?"

Well, it seems we will have to do the "chasse à l'araignée" today. As Daniel and Holly were here just before us, the place seemed relatively spider-free. Nevertheless, we should have chased the stragglers out of the house rather than wait for a rather rude arachnid to bite poor Charlie's private parts. It seems Rosie had roughly the same experience, albeit with a more discerning spider.

## Horse-riding

This afternoon we chose to go riding. Charlie had been lambasting me with requests to take him since before we even got here. All the way down in the car from Paris: "Quand est-ce qu'on fera du cheval ?", "Quel jour est-ce qu'on fera du cheval ?". Funny to see the difference in the two boys. Olivier has been dragged horse-riding with me most of his little life; he never says he does not want to come, so he must like it, but I can see he has to swallow hard every time he has to near a horse. I understand. Horses are big and powerful and highly strung. But there is nothing like a gallop along the beach or in the countryside, man and animal as one. Charlie, however, tells me he has been on a horse only once in his lifetime, and he is all for it.

I chose to take them to "Chez Valdine" at Calvignac, a little upstream from Tour de Faure. Olivier and I have been many times and for a beginner it is one of my favourite riding outlets. The route to Chez Valdine takes us near the Château de Cenevières, and we decide to visit it tomorrow.

Over the back of the Causses, at Saskia Stalmeier's riding school at Esclauzel, the PomPon Poney Club, only experienced riders are allowed out on the horses; everyone else stays in the ring and has lessons until they are deemed good enough to go out. This rule is of course a blessing when you have a good level and want to have a real ride - it is true that most holiday riding is full of first-time riders where the clients squeal or scream if ever the horse drags its hooves from a crawl to a real walk.

What I find amazing about Saskia's place is that children with absolutely no experience learn, in one hour, to do equestrian vaulting. If you do not know what this is, as I did not until Cameron, Harry and Daisy tried it, it is a type of gymnastics on horseback. The children, in one hour, learn to sit bareback on a pony while it walks, trots and canters. But not only that, they also learn to kneel and even stand backwards on the pony's back.

Saskia knows a lot more about horses than I do, so she is very probably right that the children learn a lot more about horses and balance, and therefore how to stay on them, than they would just walking among the trees for an hour.

Her school was a marvellous discovery, which I would recommend to everyone.

However, I was going riding with teenagers, and for a couple of teenagers to get their thrills a gallop was necessary. So therefore today, it was Chez Valdine for the umpteenth time. As usual, being tall I was given an enormous horse, as were the boys. I really do understand Olivier's hesitation every time he has to jump on one of these animals. Another thing I like about Chez Valdine is that Valdine herself tends to take you out. She is a friendly, down to earth woman, who allows no vouvoyer-ing.

She puts the better riders at the back, those who want to gallop, then at given moments on her chosen route, those at the back stop, let the others round a bend or two, and then we catch up at a gallop.

Charlie was very funny to watch ride - he held the reins as if he were driving a car. Absolutely not an ounce of fear in the boy. Unfortunately or luckily for him, I am not sure which and did not like to ask, his spider bite burst.

# This summer – Day 4

Although I have lived in France for years now, I am still enamoured by the outdoor markets with their wonderful-smelling fruits and fresh non-polluted vegetables. Tour de Faure has its own market during the summer months, while others are dotted all over the area. My favourite and choice for today is the market at Limognes en Quercy, which will take us past the Château de Cenevières.

## Château de Cenevières

"This charming man..." Isn't that a song? Indeed the châtelain of the Château de Cenevières is one. I have crossed paths with the charming M. de Braquilanges several times as he ushers out tourists and nevertheless gives a quick history of his castle to those who are disappointed by the closure of the gates. In fact until today I have always managed to arrive just as the castle closes for the day.

Today, however, we made the effort to arrive early, after our market outing, so therefore the gates were wide open and welcoming. Unfortunately M. de Braquilanges himself was nowhere to be seen, so his enthusiastic, well-informed and thoroughly pleasant descendants escorted us on a tour of the rooms open to the public. From what I understand, it is not always easy to keep such family heirlooms as castles in good repair, so grandchildren, nieces and nephews have to think up ingenious plans to keep out the rain such as these guided visits or seminars or weddings.

What is so nice about this castle, and many others far from big cities, is that there is a feeling of trust. The visitors are trusted not to run off with the family silver. But should they really be so? Our near disaster of the day was when Harry missed becoming the man in the iron mask by a hair's breadth...

The moral of this story is: "never be so interested in a guided visit that you do not watch what your children are doing".

Luckily we were saved by the skin of our teeth from a diplomatic incident when Alex noticed the absence of all five children. He discretely left our circle of enchanted adults and returned to the room in which he had last seen the children - to find Harry and Cameron in full-blown battle. As I am a doubting Thomas, and was not actually privy to this scene, I feel the story could have been embroidered slightly, but the story goes that the bolder children had donned armoured helmets and were brandishing imaginary lethal weapons, used many centuries ago by the ancestors of M. de Braquilanges. Thereupon Alex had to wrench Harry's head out of the helmet where it had managed to get momentarily stuck! Luckily for us, that day there were not enough of M. de Braquilanges' family members to notice our unruly mob, and Alex was able to replace the helmets in their correct places as if they had never been touched.

As with many castles built over various centuries, it is an interesting architectural mixture. Some buildings go back to the 13th century when a château fort stood on the hill at Cenevières dominating the valley. Then over the next three centuries, other less fortified buildings were added. From the terrace we can now appreciate the wonderful views out over the river Lot, without worrying who might be sailing down the river to attack.

Everyone we met who worked in the château was pleased to be helping the patriarch of their family keep their family jewel and went about their task of host enthusiastically and in a welcoming manner. This feeling of being welcome has been reinforced in my memory by my favourite part of the visit - our guide allowed me to enter the alchemist's room although it was supposed to be closed to the public today. As I have said, old, dilapidated buildings fire my imagination, so being allowed into such an amazingly medieval room, full of ancient thought patterns and hopes of glory permitted me to live a dream. The drawings on the walls had evidently seen time pass, and were reminiscent of the magic that I feel is associated with alchemy.

I am always astonished to think that such a large place in society was given to such an incomprehensible quest so many years ago. But perhaps my incomprehension is because with hindsight we know we cannot force lead to become gold. I also associate alchemy with the seedier, magical side of it; and human beings' greedy wish to turn everything to gold, which poor King Midas must have regretted bitterly. However, despite my misgivings about the subject, it would seem that medieval European alchemists made some useful discoveries, which later gave rise to modern chemistry, and it took many centuries until the gold-making processes of alchemists were finally discredited. Perhaps alchemy will one day make a comeback.

## Le Rocher des aigles

On this fifth day there was no time for my usual quiet morning moment as everyone else sleeps. Today we all decided to get up early, as we had a long drive ahead of us to the "Rocher des aigles" at Rocamadour up in the North West of the Lot.

I was quite happy to take our friends up to see the show, although Pascal, Olivier and I have already been several times, as I have never grown tired of it. Apart from the obvious fact that the show put on by birds of prey, varieties of parrots and their trainers is excellent, the most amazing thing for me as a British person, is that you can bring your dog to watch these kites, vultures, eagles and falcons fly. Surely this just would not happen in the United Kingdom? Our dog is after all a natural hunter; and vice-versa for the birds.

My fears were confirmed when Oscar broke away from his lead with the excitement of it all. After having spent half an hour eyeing each other up - birds of prey versus Westie - it was Oscar who made the first attempt to get together with the birds. As I ran after the dog, fearful and embarrassed, the announcer shouted through his microphone, "Do not worry, Madame, none of the birds has strong enough claws to carry off your little dog." I was so relieved to hear them worry about the dog! Personally, I was having visions of Oscar's hunting instincts coming back (true enough he has never so much as touched a defenceless rabbit, but...) and closing his small but powerful jaws around the neck of a rare and beautiful eagle (grrr, shake, shake, crunch... dead eagle). Wouldn't that have been terrible. As it was, I managed to get Oscar back on his lead before there was any agro from either side.

For those of you who think it is a pity to have caged, captured birds, it would seem to me that these birds are happy with their life as actors. They circle high in the sky waiting to swoop down when they are called for their turn to show off. The birds fly between trainers on opposite stages doing their acrobatics.

Some catch food in flight, some catch fish in a shallow pool of water or show us that they know how to use a stone to break open an egg. There are also many brightly coloured parrots, macaws and cockatoos who take part in the show.

Last time we were there one hopped from head to head to delight the children in the audience; this time we were asked to sit on the ground with our legs outstretched so that a small bird of prey could walk across them. Still as an adult, I love all contact with animals, so the chance to touch or be touched by a bird of prey or parrot is marvellous to me. I have picked up koalas and fed apple to wallabies in Australia, shared my sandwich with a weka in New Zealand, given fish to dolphins and touched silky bat rays in California, picked up a lovely squishy baby alligator in Florida - yes the underneath is squishy - ridden camels, touched surprisingly hairy elephant trunks... you name it, if I'm given the chance to touch it I will take it. So here at this wonderful show at Rocamadour one of my favourite parts is when there is real contact between a bird and the audience.

The purpose of this bird park is not to ensnare the animals who live there but to use them as ambassadors to convince we human beings that we should protect their natural habitat. The parrots were all born in zoos so do not know any other life. And many of the residents have in fact been brought in from the wild for mating, the descendants taught to fend for themselves, then set free again in their natural habitat. They are not permanent captives.

The show we saw today was magnificent, but I have to admit to a particular penchant for the "chouettes" and the "hiboux", who did not take part in the display. The French language makes the difference between two types of owls. First of all, the hibou, which would appear to have cute little ears perched on the top of its head (in fact it is a bouquet of feathers), and second, the chouette, which has a perfect oval at the top of its head. There are all sorts of owls here. All are beautiful. All with the most wonderful large round eyes that blink at you from time to time. They come from all over the world. Even the little New Zealand morepork is there, its little round head just the right size to fit inside the arch of the corrugated iron ceiling of its cage.

## Canoeing on the Célé

Got to keep those teenagers moving, so we organised some canoeing on the River Célé today. Just Pascal and I, Olivier and Charlie; one canoe for each pair. Our friends went all the way back up to Rocamadour to visit that medieval masterpiece and then cool off in the watery caves of the nearby Gouffre de Padirac; but we have been many times already, so decided that some fresh air and sport was called for instead. We packed our sandwiches to have for lunch at a chosen spot on the banks of the Célé, and parted ways with our friends at Cabrerets.

The canoe company, left us upriver at Marcilhac sur Célé, with the canoes we had hired and various other tourists, to make our way back down the river to the point where it flows into the River Lot at Cabrerets. We plastered sun cream on our teenagers' arms and backs, then stuffed our sandwiches, shoes and mobiles into our plastic barrels, which we then strapped into the canoe in case we capsized and lost all of our belongings. How one could possibly capsize on this slow-flowing river, which is only inches deep at this time of year seems difficult to believe, but it is better to be safe than sorry.

On such a beautiful hot, sunny day, this peaceful float down the river with its wonderful landscape of green trees and white cliffs is a must. It is not an experienced canoe-goer's idea of a challenge - white-water rafters beware, do not bother with the Célé in August. Nevertheless, we quickly became aware, when Oscar, who hated the canoe, decided to jump off and make it back to the bank, that the river might not be quite as slow-moving as its smooth surface and shallow depth had made us believe. Oscar was immediately left far behind as the canoes continued their descent without him. We had to paddle hard against the current to get back to him, pick him up by the scruff of the neck and drag him back in. At that point we began to realise the force of the river even at this calm, relatively rainless period of the year.

He did learn his lesson and did not try to get back to the bank alone again. If there is one thing Oscar dislikes it is to be left alone.

At one point, there is a tight meander where the water becomes suddenly effervescent as it rushes past several visible rocks. We were just about to brave these rapids, when up came the two boys, paddling like their lives depended on it, so that they could overtake us.

Sometimes we see something coming but have no control over it... I saw it... I nevertheless started screaming at them, no doubt hysterically, to stay behind us... but it was too late.

Just as we were rounding the bend at the fastest speed we had been at so far, bang came the adolescents, straight into the side of our canoe. The force of their canoe pushed our nose up onto what at first appeared to be the bank. Unfortunately for us, however, it was not a bank, but a huge heap of branches and tree stumps, washed up there by the current. Our canoe's nose stuck between the branches, then the back whip-lashed round in the current and tried to drag us backwards down the river. With Pascal at the helm rather than my spindly little arms, this should have worked out quite well; he would usually have got us turned around and back in the right direction.

However, the nose of the canoe could not get free and we were off balance. I remember this accident vividly, each second imprinted in my memory. Next, the whole canoe turned over. Pascal fell out and was up and out of the water in a flash. I, in what seemed like hours, was stuck under the canoe. I was luckily out of the canoe and I was vertical, but the canoe was above me. The water pulled me backwards downstream, but the canoe followed me, enclosing me in the water. I was trapped under the canoe and could not get out. It was all over in seconds no doubt, but my legs were ripped to shreds by stones on the bottom of river, bruises already showing, and I had had one of those rare near-death experiences where everything went into slow motion. Not only that, the sunglasses I had especially run out to buy just before going on holiday were gone.

As I got over the shock, I could see some very shame-faced teenagers half-way down to the next meander in the river, pretending they were looking for my sunglasses there, not willing to come back up river to apologise. I knew they were sorry though. And they did express their regret once Pascal had enforced his wish of this... All's well that ends well. Their faces were punishment enough.

Lesson of the day: never underestimate the power of water.

## Cabrerets, its potter, the Château du Diable and its legend of the white goat

Albeit that my legs were covered in scratches and bruises after our little canoeing incident, I have never spent a holiday in the Lot without dropping by the local potter in Cabrerets. Therefore, as we were in the vicinity it seemed a good time to go. Our house in Paris is already inundated with pottery from Cabrerets and St Cirq, but I feel I have not been on holiday if I do not make this little pilgrimage.

On the way there, we drive past the Château du Diable (Devil's castle), which has been a ruin since many a year. Like the cliff dwellings at Bouziès, which are troglodyte constructions chiselled out of the rock face of the cliff above the river Lot, this castle is constructed in the same fashion above the river Célé. Etched out of the rock many centuries ago, legend has it that in 745 it was inhabited by the Duke of Aquitaine. It would seem that the seigneur brought death upon himself as his political ideas went against those of the king at the time.

King Pépin le Bref, the father of the great King and Emperor Charlemagne, wanted unity for France, whereas the seigneur of the Château du Diable wanted independence for Aquitaine. As was the custom in those days, the discord was solved simply - by ending his life.

It is, however, difficult to have much sympathy for the fellow once we have heard the Legend of the White Goat, which haunts this ruin.

To situate the story, imagine this fortress many centuries ago. Cut out of the rock high above the Célé, it was originally about 90 metres long and 30 metres high, with walls about three metres thick, flanked by two round towers, one of which is still visible against the rock. On the rock face was painted a dragon and a red devil, spitting flames to fend off the enemy...

On the night of Christmas 745, a young goat shepherdess came to the castle to ask for the seigneur's help because her grandmother was dying of hunger. The girl, although dressed in rags, was noticeably very pretty, so the seigneur said he would help her if she would become mistress of the manor. As he approached the girl, while all the other men in the room were laughing in an uproariously wicked way, the girl understood what he had in mind and preferred to escape through a window. The pretty shepherdess, Mariette, jumped out of the window, into the cold wintry waters of the Célé and drowned in the river on that Christmas night 745, her last words being "Jesus, Mary".

It is said that these evil ways were inspired by the devil who haunted the place and was painted on the outside wall. Mariette's tormentor joined her 23 years later, clubbed to death, then thrown out of the same window into the river. It is said that the ghost of the seigneur can be seen some nights. And on nights of the full moon, a little white goat can be seen at the top of the rocky cliffs that line the Célé.

# This summer – Day 7

No holiday in the Lot is complete without a trip to the main town of the département, Cahors. A visit of the old town and the beautiful cathedral, named after Saint Stephen (Saint Etienne in French) is a must. Cahors is set in a U-turn meander of the river Lot which lends to much geographical confusion for new arrivals. The most famous of the bridges that crosses the river here is the Valentré Bridge.

## The myths and legends of Cahors – le Pont Valentré

Undoubtedly, the inhabitants of the Middle Ages had a thing about the devil. The minute anything went wrong back in those days, he got blamed for it. It seems the building of the beautiful Pont Valentré (Valentré Bridge) that spans the Lot at Cahors was begun about seven hundred years ago (in 1308), but then that old devil intervened, and it was another seventy years before the bridge was finally finished. The legend goes that the first master craftsman in charge of the building of the bridge simply was not up to the job. Therefore, a new man was put in his place, who made great promises about the deadline. Everything was going smoothly until one day one of the workers fell from the scaffolding, broke his neck and died. Very soon afterwards, the river flooded, and from there on in everything went wrong.

Medieval man felt generally terrified by this chain of events and the overseer, after having been so proud of his good work and progress, felt shame-faced. As a last resort, this God-fearing man went to an old ugly witch with only one eye and asked for her help. She told him that only the devil could help him. Well, he was not very happy about this, but really could not see any way out of it. As it was, before he had even made up a plan, when he was dragging himself to work the next morning along the banks of the river, the devil suddenly emerged from the river with his horns and claws and trident. At that point, the overseer made a deal with the devil that he would give him his soul if he got the bridge finished by the deadline. Of course nothing could be simpler for the devil, who therefore accepted this proposition with vehemence.

However, the overseer had a little trick up his sleeve and asked the devil to help out personally with the building of the bridge, to which the devil once again agreed. As the work came to an end, the devil appeared and was given his task - he was to bring water to a worker at the top of the central tower who needed it to complete his task. What could be easier for the devil!

As it was the clever overseer gave the devil a sieve in which to carry the water. Well even the devil had problems with that, and did not manage to complete the deal. In anger, then, he dived back into the river (where he had first been when the overseer met him) and was never seen again. However, the next morning the overseer realised that one of the corner stones of the central tower had fallen.

He found it complete with the scratches of a five-fingered devil's hand, at the bottom of the tower, showing that the devil had tried to destroy the bridge. To confound the devil, therefore, the overseer replaced it with a stone from sacred ground...

The devil did his best to climb up the tower and dislodge that stone, but however hard he tried he could not manage it... If you look up at the central tower now, you can see a sculpture of the devil himself, put there during 19th century renovations to remind us of the medieval legend.

## The weir

On this last day of this year's all too short holiday in the Lot, I finally got the wish I had wished on my first day - a lazy afternoon by the waterside.

Today, in this wonderful house where, when I am the hostess, there are no particular roles for women or men, inviters or invitees, Alex had decided to make us a barbecue lunch. That meant freedom to sit in Daniel's favourite place and read while it was being prepared. The other tradition in this house is that the dishes are done by all children over 12ish. As usual, the little children, still not dextrous enough for this task would cheerfully have completed it, so they run around under the feet of the teenagers, trying to help them. However, for our 16 year old, Charlie, washing and drying dishes was a new concept.

Initially horrified at this swapping of traditional roles, he accepted it well, particularly as they got to play blaring teenager music on Daniel's brilliant sound system at the same time.

During this moment, not conducive to those who have a sensitive ear, Pascal and I were able to toddle off to our secret pebbled beach for a final top up of our sun tans, and swim in the river. Olivier and Charlie would catch up with us later, while Alex and Rosie would plump for an afternoon at the camping site beach, where the children can play and swim safely in the river under the vigilance of the lifeguard.

Our secret beach, which is now also your secret beach, is located just after the weir. The water flows fast here, so is more dangerous for children and little dogs like Oscar.

We all love to wade out to where the river flows fast, lie down and let the water take us off downstream. Oscar, despite his small size and relative strength, loves to do this too. He is a brave little chap, because although the water is so shallow that we scrape our bottoms along the river bed, Oscar, with his short little legs, is out of his depth, completely incapable of fighting the current. However, he has understood that the current brings him back to shore a little further downstream. So we all do it together.

On this final day in this little corner of paradise that I fell in love with so many years ago now, our oldest adolescent also fell in love. He saved a very beautiful young girl from the turbulent flow at the weir, and fell hook, line and sinker more deeply in love with her than the river he had saved her from. That pure and simple first-time love that only the young can feel.

Like my first time in the Lot.

## Watercolors & Illustrations

Texts by Helen-Anne Shields
Watercolors by Pascal Margat
Illustrations by Véronique Bonnel